Cheetahs
in Focus

Rob Waring, *Series Editor*

HEINLE
CENGAGE Learning

Australia • Brazil • Japan • Korea • Mexico • Singapore • Spain • United Kingdom • United States

Words to Know

This story is set in Africa. It takes place in the Moremi [mɔrəmi] Wildlife Reserve in Botswana [bɔtswɑnɑ]; however, the story starts in Johannesburg [dʒoʊhɑnəsbɜrg], South Africa.

A **In the Wildlife Reserve.** Here are some animals you will find in the story. Label the picture with words from the box.

a buffalo	giraffes	reedbucks
a cheetah	a hyena	zebra

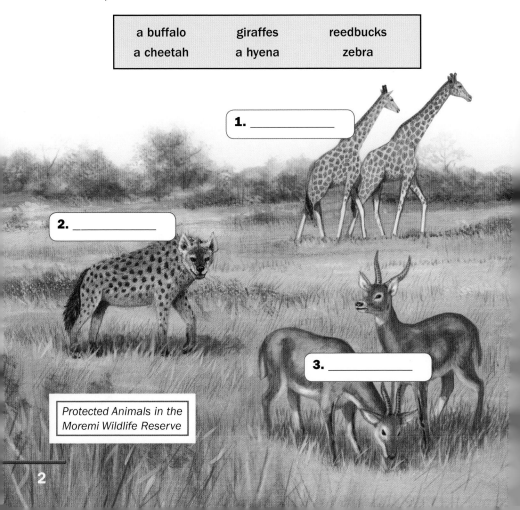

1. _____

2. _____

3. _____

Protected Animals in the Moremi Wildlife Reserve

B **Cheetahs.** Read the definitions. Then complete the paragraph with the correct forms of the words.

extinct: no longer in existence
habitat: the natural area in which an animal or plant normally lives
predator: an animal that lives by killing and eating other animals
prey: animals killed for food by other animals
species: a specific group of living things that have similar characteristics

Cheetahs are the fastest land animals alive and one of nature's most dangerous (1) _____. When hunting, they are able to chase their (2) _____ at very high speeds. Unfortunately, this amazing (3) _____ of animal is in serious danger. About 100 years ago, there were nearly 100,000 cheetahs in the wild, but after years of losing their (4) _____, it is estimated that fewer than 12,000 remain. Cheetahs are in danger of becoming (5) _____ and soon there may be no more left in natural areas.

6. _____

4. _____

5. _____

A cheetah running at full speed while it chases its prey is one of the most remarkably beautiful sights in the natural world. With an astonishing ability to **sprint**[1] from zero to eighty kilometers an hour in just three seconds, the cheetah is the fastest animal on land. When this giant cat is running at top speed, it can reach speeds of almost 100 kilometers an hour. For any animal unlucky enough to become a cheetah's prey, the drama doesn't often last long. Nothing can escape a cheetah at full sprint. It's only a matter of time, and the chances of survival decrease with each step. If the animal makes one slip, the cheetah's powerful legs cut the distance between predator and prey. Once the creature is caught though, death is thankfully quick as the cheetah grips the neck of its prey firmly in its mouth and waits for the animal to stop fighting.

Unfortunately, the cheetah may be facing an early end for itself as well. This beautiful, shy animal is in serious danger of becoming extinct. It is estimated that fewer than 12,000 cheetahs remain in existence in the wild today. For some, the thought of losing such an incredible animal is unthinkable. In order to help, National Geographic has sent a team on an assignment into the Moremi Wildlife Reserve in Botswana. Their goal is to help save these magnificent creatures by **capturing**[2] them on camera.

---

[1]**sprint:** run very fast for a short distance
[2]**capture:** record or take a picture of something

 CD 1, Track 01

Johannesburg, South Africa, is the starting point for many expeditions into the Okavango Delta.

The city of Johannesburg, South Africa, is the final stop before the team's journey deep into the wilds of Africa. They have come to photograph cheetahs for National Geographic Magazine, and heading the **expedition**[3] is Chris Johns, who has been a photographer for more than 25 years. Chris has been planning this trip for a long time, and accompanying him is local guide, Dave Hamman. Dave has lived in southern Africa for most of his life and knows the region very well. His knowledge will be useful as the two men head more than 800 kilometers north into Botswana and the wonderful Okavango Delta.

The two men need to use trucks for their journey due to the rough land through which they must drive. They take off from Johannesburg and move into heavy rain as they wind their way towards 'the bush,' which is the term commonly used to describe land far away from towns and cities in Africa. Later, as the trucks drive along rough roads and through extremely wild land, one thing becomes very obvious; their destination in the Moremi Wildlife Reserve is about as far into the bush as one can get.

---

[3]**expedition:** a journey organized for a special purpose

The Moremi Reserve is a truly magical place, and is well worth the long and difficult journey to get there. It seems that Africa's entire animal kingdom resides in the region and greets Chris and Dave as they drive through the large open plain. Groups of buffaloes can be seen cooling themselves in the mud left after the heavy showers. Zebras walk quietly along an unseen path, and elephant families are easily viewed from the rough dirt road. Even a giraffe makes an appearance, walking slowly against a brilliant red sky as the sun sets on the horizon.

Although the day is coming to an end, Chris and Dave continue their drive late into the evening. They need to be far into the wilderness to begin their task: finding cheetahs to photograph. They realize that in the large area of the Moremi Reserve, finding these animals may be quite complicated. They also know that looking for cheetahs is a waiting game, and great **patience**[4] is required in order to observe them in their natural habitat. After the long journey, the two men are left to wonder how long they must wait before they catch sight of an animal. They have traveled so far for a chance to photograph a cheetah, but they must remember, there is no promise of success.

---

[4]**patience:** the ability to accept discomfort, pain, or troubles while waiting calmly

The next day, the men are up early to begin their search for cheetahs. Chris and Dave know from experience that it may be a long and difficult hunt. Chris explains the realities of looking for these rare creatures: "You can't just drive out there and order up a cheetah. It doesn't happen like that. You know that it could take days, [or] weeks."

The men set off on their day's journey, but then something unexpected occurs; the team spots what they are looking for almost immediately. "I don't believe this," laughs Dave in surprise when he sees a female and five of her young walking near their truck. During all of his years in the bush, Dave has never located so many cheetahs this quickly. Both men feel extremely lucky. When they began this journey, this is exactly what they had been hoping for.

The discovery is especially promising for Chris. If he is able to follow the cheetah family for a period of time, he may be able to tell an important story. He feels that cheetahs are a kind of ecological analogy for some of Africa's most complicated conservation issues. He explains: "Cheetahs are a **metaphor**[5] for some of Africa's conservation problems. Because cheetahs need [a wide] range, and they are a good way to explain to people that loss of habitat means the potential loss of species. And it's possible that in my lifetime cheetahs could become extinct in the wild, and that's—to me—a **tragedy**[6] that's **unspeakable**."[7]

---

[5]**metaphor:** a thing that represents another; a symbol
[6]**tragedy:** a sad event; a terrible misfortune
[7]**unspeakable:** so bad or shocking it cannot be expressed in words

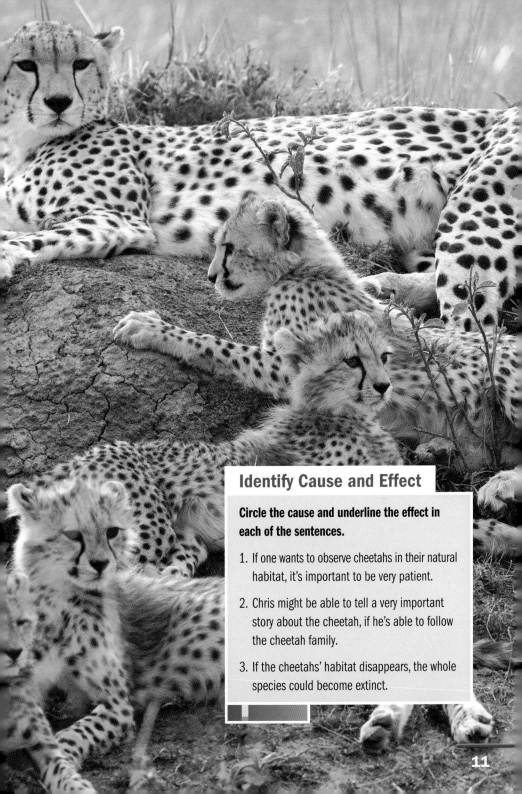

Identify Cause and Effect

Circle the cause and underline the effect in each of the sentences.

1. If one wants to observe cheetahs in their natural habitat, it's important to be very patient.

2. Chris might be able to tell a very important story about the cheetah, if he's able to follow the cheetah family.

3. If the cheetahs' habitat disappears, the whole species could become extinct.

Luckily, the Moremi Wildlife Reserve in Botswana has offered Chris one of the last windows into the natural world of the cheetah. Cheetahs are very **cautious**[8] by nature, and shy of humans. As Chris and Dave drive around the newly found group, the animals look nervously at the truck. Finally, when the truck passes by too closely, one cheetah quickly gets out of the way, unsure what to think of the large machine.

It will take a while for the cheetahs to trust Chris, but if he succeeds, he knows he'll be able to take the photographs he really wants. Every photographer knows that the most valuable shots are those of a cheetah pursuing and killing its prey, or a 'kill sequence.' Chris explains: "We know there are certain things that a cheetah story has to have. One of the most important things it has to have—which is an incredibly difficult thing to get—is a kill sequence, and you're always looking for that picture."

_____

[8]**cautious:** careful; concerned about danger

Cheetahs are capable of **tremendous**[9] bursts of speed, and have the capacity to gain speed more quickly than a sports car. However, while these amazing cats can reach almost 100 kilometers an hour, they aren't able to continue running at high speeds for long periods of time. They usually sprint in short intervals and can't maintain such speeds for more than 200 to 300 meters. As a result, despite having a close chase, they sometimes don't catch their prey if it is able to run for a longer time.

Later in the day, Chris and Dave actually get a chance to watch the female cheetah as she chases a reedbuck; however, she unfortunately fails to catch it. Cheetahs must make a kill every few days. With the extra burden of five **cubs**,[10] this mother must make a kill soon in order to provide enough food for all of them or they could die. After missing the reedbuck, the mother is exhausted, and her cubs are still hungry. The two men drive back to their camp, leaving the cheetah family to rest in the shade of the trees, away from the extremely hot sun.

---

[9]**tremendous:** huge or great; in large amounts
[10]**cub:** one of the young of certain wild animals

The next day, Chris and Dave excitedly return to where they last saw the cheetah family. Unfortunately, an even bigger—and more disappointing—surprise than they had earlier is waiting for them. The mother and her cubs are gone. The men are obviously upset as they realize that the mother has probably taken the cubs a considerable distance away in order to protect them. The two men will need to start looking for the cheetah family all over again if they want to get those important photos.

Chris and Dave orient themselves to their surroundings and start driving across the huge open plain of the Moremi. As they do so, the size of their job becomes apparent. The chances of quickly finding the cheetah family again in this 4,800-square-kilometer wildlife reserve are very slim. This kind of work certainly requires a great deal of patience. It's a challenge which Chris emphasizes some days later, when they are still tirelessly searching for the family. "We still haven't seen the mother with five cubs for several days now," he says. "The challenge is to keep your **concentration**,[11] to constantly look. I mean, we're looking for at least eight to ten hours a day."

---

[11]**concentration:** the ability to focus one's thoughts on a particular notion or task

The tiring and difficult search for the cheetah family turns from days into a week. The two men look everywhere across the endless open lands of the reserve. They scan everything from heavy bushes to open grasslands, hoping to catch sight of the mother. It's difficult for them not to lose hope that they will find the family again, but then, suddenly, their efforts become worth it; they see the mother. "There!" says Dave, "Let's go, let's go!" he adds as Chris scans the grass to find the female cheetah. "Did you see her?" Chris asks. "Yeah!" replies Dave, "She's in the grass, just down [there]." At last, Chris spots the animal as well and the two men jump quickly into their truck to head over to the long-lost family.

As they near the cheetah family, the men can see that it is the same mother they watched over a week ago and she looks fine. Chris must now wait to see if the mother cheetah will let him back into her trust so that he can get close enough to photograph her hunt. Only she can decide if and when he will be allowed to watch. While they wait, Chris takes some still photographs of the family from a distance. Both men are extremely happy that they have found the family once again.

Chris's opportunity for shooting a kill sequence presents itself later in the morning as the mother is resting in the shade. Suddenly, she sits up and her ears move slightly; she's watching and listening carefully because she's seen something in the bush. The men soon spot what she is looking at: two reedbucks. Chris and Dave watch and wait as the mother cheetah silently observes her prey. With her cubs hidden away, the brave hunter moves closer and closer to her target. Chris pulls his huge video camera from its case in preparation to shoot the scene. The cheetah may start chasing the reedbuck at any moment.

Then, suddenly, it happens. The mother sets off at full speed after the reedbuck, "There she goes! There she goes!" says Chris excitedly as they take off at top speed in their truck to follow her as she hunts. "Hang on!" Dave shouts as the open truck speeds over the uneven ground of the grassland. The two must drive as quickly as possible in order to pursue the fastest animal on four legs. While Dave tries to handle the truck during the rough ride, Chris must try to hang on and avoid falling out of the moving vehicle. Incredibly, he manages to take photographs of the cheetah's hunt as he does so.

Suddenly, the great hunt is over. The mother has caught one of the reedbuck. She will be able to feed herself and her cubs today. "Got 'em! Good job, girl," says Chris to the female cheetah, "Well done!" He then adds, "She's a good hunter. She's a real[ly] good hunter," as she settles down with her newly caught prey. Chris then takes the opportunity to photograph a sight that humans very rarely see—a cheetah killing its prey.

In typical cheetah style, the mother **chokes**[12] her prey, fixing her teeth firmly around the reedbuck's neck until the animal is dead. Then, once she has killed the reedbuck, the cheetah takes time to recover from her fast sprint. As she does so, she continues to glance around nervously. Chris explains that this is a time when the female cheetah is most **vulnerable**.[13] At this point, another predator, such as a hyena, could easily slip in to feed on the reedbuck— and attack her cubs. "It's a vulnerable time because if a hyena or another predator moved in on her here, she could be **ambushed**,"[14] he says. "She is going to be very cautious."

---

[12]**choke:** cut off an air supply by applying firm pressure to the neck
[13]**vulnerable:** exposed or unprotected
[14]**ambush:** attack from a hidden position

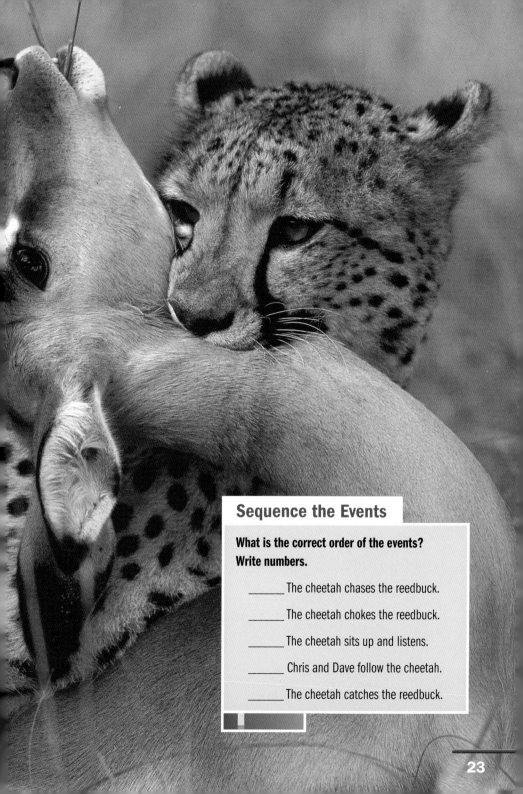

Sequence the Events

What is the correct order of the events? Write numbers.

_____ The cheetah chases the reedbuck.

_____ The cheetah chokes the reedbuck.

_____ The cheetah sits up and listens.

_____ Chris and Dave follow the cheetah.

_____ The cheetah catches the reedbuck.

Finally, satisfied for the moment that no other predators are in the area, the female begins to make a series of short barking sounds. She is calling her cubs to come meet her for their meal. The cubs approach cautiously from a nearby group of trees to join their mother. Once the young animals reach the dead reedbuck, they start eating hungrily. It takes the mother and cubs an hour to eat their share of the reedbuck, which allows Chris plenty of time to take photographs.

The mother and cubs are finally trusting Chris more than he ever expected, and it's a wonderful experience. "It's amazing that the cheetahs are letting me this close. These are the pictures I've been waiting for for ten years," he says excitedly. The animals allow the photographer to get very close to them as they feed on the reedbuck. Amazingly, he's able to capture the whole scene with his camera.

Dave agrees that this is a very special moment, but he knows that a lot of very hard work made it happen. "You only see things like this if you're extremely lucky, but also patient," he says. "How many hours have we spent with these cheetahs now to actually get this far? You know, you just have to put in the time to get the results." Finally, all of their patience has brought the expedition the results they had been waiting to achieve, but there is still one more surprise ahead of them …

Chris and Dave stay near the family to observe them over time. Each day, mother and cubs open up more to the humans, and allow the men to get closer. Then finally, one day while Chris is photographing the animals from a short distance, something truly wonderful happens. As Chris clicks away on his camera, one of the cheetahs focuses its attention on him. Chris pauses in his photography as the animal comes nearer. The cheetah seems to be curious about the large black object that's making strange noises —and the man behind it. Chris freezes in amazement as the animal walks directly up to his camera and begins to carefully smell the huge lens, perhaps in an effort to identify the unusual scent. Then—even more to the team's amazement—the animal moves around to the side of the camera and begins to lick the photographer's hand!

The experience has definitely had a significant effect on Chris. "That was a fantastic experience, for me [it was] one of the **highlights**[15] of my life," he says. Chris now feels that he has a special responsibility to communicate the endangered status of this beautiful animal to the world. He wants to show how important—and threatened— these animals are through his series of photographs and the accompanying National Geographic article. "She's just given me a tremendous privilege, one of the finest privileges of my life," he explains. "So with that privilege goes a great deal of responsibility, I think, on my part." Hopefully, Chris can fulfill this responsibility by bringing the endangerment of these animals into worldwide focus. Maybe his actions will help save the cheetahs of the Okavango, and the world.

---

[15]**highlight:** a great or special point

Summarize

Imagine that you were on the cheetah expedition. Write or talk about what you saw and explain how you felt.

After You Read

1. What will the National Geographic team do on their trip to Botswana to help preserve the cheetah?
   A. teach individuals about cheetahs
   B. help with local conservation efforts
   C. take photographs of cheetahs
   D. research a way to help cheetahs

2. What is the main purpose of page 7?
   A. to compare Johannesburg to the Okavango Delta
   B. to describe the goal of the expedition
   C. to explain that the weather is unreliable
   D. to introduce the team members

3. On their first day at the Moremi Reserve, the team sees each of the following EXCEPT:
   A. zebras
   B. a giraffe
   C. cheetahs
   D. elephants

4. Which word on page 10 means 'precisely'?
   A. immediately
   B. exactly
   C. potential
   D. possible

5. Which is true about a cheetah?
   A. It only eats twice a month.
   B. It's slower than a sports car.
   C. It never gets tired.
   D. It can maintain high speeds for a short time.

6. The team thinks the cheetah family probably left the spot where they saw them:
   A. for safety reasons
   B. to find food
   C. because of the weather
   D. to find shade

7. In paragraph 2 on page 18, 'they' in 'As they near' refers to:
   A. the cheetah family
   B. the cheetah cubs
   C. a family of reedbuck
   D. Chris and Dave

8. Chris is waiting for the mother cheetah to start chasing
   _____ prey.
   A. her
   B. a
   C. that
   D. two

9. What part of the reedbuck's body does the cheetah bite to choke
   the animal?
   A. back
   B. head
   C. neck
   D. leg

10. Which of the following is a good heading for paragraph 1 on page 25?
    A. Man Freezes in Amusement
    B. Cheetah Attacks Photographer
    C. Cub Takes Picture of Man
    D. Cheetah Offers Greeting

11. What opinion does Dave express on page 25?
    A. It's impossible to get a cheetah to trust a human.
    B. The expedition has not been easy.
    C. Chris is a great photographer.
    D. Another animal will steal the reedbuck.

12. What will Chris probably do after this expedition?
    A. teach others about cheetahs
    B. buy a book about photography
    C. give the cheetah family some food
    D. start working at a zoo

Understanding
EXTINCTION

A species is considered extinct when careful scientific surveys show that the last individual of that species has died. The loss of many species of plants and animals has been attributed to changes in climate, genetic weaknesses, and human activities such as hunting and environmental destruction. Studies have shown that almost all living things will eventually become extinct. In fact, more than 99 percent of the species that have ever lived on Earth have now disappeared permanently. Although this sounds like a terrible situation, it is important to understand that the earth seems to recover from the loss of great numbers of species. In many cases, replacement species emerge over time; however, extinction does decrease the diversity of life on the planet in the short term. These replacement species often require recovery periods of millions of years.

Human beings have had a huge impact on the extinction rates of various species. Therefore, scientists have recently begun to examine humankind's effects on the numbers of species that have become extinct. Through the use of geographical and biological research, a 'background extinction rate' has been established. These figures show the numbers of species which have disappeared during specific time periods. By comparing rates of extinction before and after human existence, researchers were able to discover the exact effects of humankind on nature. Studies now cite that the extinction rates after human life began are 100 to 1,000 times greater than before human influence on Earth. Future rates are forecasted to be even higher. This demonstrates the tremendous negative impact that human activity is having on extinction rates.

The Indian tiger is one of the few species of tigers that has not become extinct.

10 Extinct Animals

	Animal	Date of Extinction	Probable Cause of Extinction
1	Tyrannosaurus Rex (dinosaur)	65 million years ago	Climate Change
2	Quagga (zebra species)	1883	Human Activity (hunting)
3	Tasmanian Tiger	1936	Disease, Human Activity (hunting, loss of habitat, introduction of new species)
4	Stellar's Sea Cow	1768	Human Activity (hunting)
5	Irish Deer	7,700 years ago	Climate Change, Human Activity (hunting), loss of habitat
6	Caspian Tiger	circa* 1970	Human Activity (hunting)
7	Aurochs (a large cow)	1627	Human Activity (hunting, loss of habitat)
8	Great Auk (a flightless bird)	1844	Human Activity (hunting)
9	Cave Lion	2,000–10,000 years ago	Human Activity (hunting, loss of habitat and prey)
10	Dodo (a flightless bird)	circa* 1650	Human Activity (hunting, loss of habitat, introduction of new species)

*circa = approximately

Scientists are currently researching methods of dealing with this astonishing trend. As individuals, educators, and governments try to manage species survival, one key factor they find is that without help, some of the world's species cannot survive. In addition, scientists must learn to make difficult decisions based on incomplete information. They must also deal with groups that may have a vested interest in not protecting certain species. For example, people interested in developing oil fields in the Arctic may not think the protection of the wildlife in the region is of primary importance.

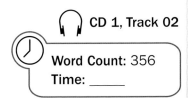

CD 1, Track 02

Word Count: 356
Time: _____

Vocabulary List

ambush (22)
buffalo (2, 8)
capture (4, 25)
cautious (13, 22, 25)
cheetah (2, 3, 4, 7, 8, 10, 11, 13, 14, 17, 18, 21, 22, 23, 25, 26, 27)
choke (22, 23)
concentration (17)
cub (14, 17, 21, 22, 25, 26)
expedition (6, 7, 25, 27)
extinct (3, 4, 10)
giraffe (2, 8)
habitat (3, 8, 10, 11)
highlight (26)
hyena (2, 22)
metaphor (10)
patience (8, 11, 17, 25)
predator (3, 4, 22, 25)
prey (3, 4, 13, 14, 21, 22)
reedbuck (2, 14, 21, 22, 23, 25)
species (3, 10, 11)
sprint (4, 14, 22)
tremendous (14, 26)
tragedy (10)
unspeakable (10)
vulnerable (22)
zebra (2, 8)